Devotional Life in the Wesleyan Tradition

DEVOTIONAL LIFE
IN THE
WESLEYAN
TRADITION

Steve Harper

THE UPPER ROOM
Nashville, Tennessee

DEVOTIONAL LIFE IN THE WESLEYAN TRADITION

Cover Design and Transparency: Steve Laughbaum
Book Design: Harriette Bateman
First printing: October, 1983(7)
Second printing: April, 1984(5)
Third printing: May 1986(3)
Library of Congress Catalog Card Number: 83-50521
ISBN: 0-8358-0467-4

Printed in the United States of America

To
Frank and Nellie Baker,
who have shown me a living Wesleyanism

Contents

Introduction

Two interesting factors are converging at this moment in the church. First, there is a genuine renaissance in Wesley Studies. Materials for scholarly research and lay enrichment are adding significantly to our knowledge and appreciation of John Wesley as a serious theologian and relevant model for personal and church renewal.

At the same time a new emphasis upon spiritual formation is taking place. It is clear that we cannot be the church apart from a deep and comprehensive practice of the devotional life. No amount of programming and structuring can substitute for personal and corporate spiritual vitality. Resources are increasing to help individuals and churches grow in this essential area.

This book is an attempt to contribute both to Wesley Studies and to spiritual formation. In it I hope to show that the heart of Wesley's life and ministry was his all-encompassing commitment to the devotional life. I hope to use his principles and practices as examples for us to follow today as we make our way forward in the spiritual life. To the extent that the book helps you to grow in the grace and knowledge of Jesus Christ, it will truly be devotional life in the Wesleyan tradition.

Dr. Steve Harper
Asbury Theological Seminary
Wilmore, Kentucky

Chapter One

John Wesley: Man of Devotion

"O BEGIN! Fix some part of every day for private exercises. . . . Whether you like it or no, read and pray daily. It is for your life; there is no other way: else you will be a trifler all your days."[1] These words of John Wesley, written to one of his itinerant preachers, show the importance of the devotional life.

Even today many in the Wesleyan tradition are aware of his long-standing commitment to Christian devotion. We know of his practice of early rising and perhaps several of the devotional works he used. But often that is the extent of our knowledge. Consequently, Wesley's example is of little concrete help to us as we wrestle with our own spiritual formation.

This is unfortunate. Wesley's devotional life can be a rich source of help and inspiration to us as we search for our own particular patterns of devotion. This book is an attempt to bring to light some facets of Wesleyan devotion which can still serve to enrich our relationship with God. The particular focus of the book is on the means of grace, which formed the basis of Wesley's devotional practices. However, as we begin it is important to know why we are looking to John Wesley as a relevant guide for our devotional pilgrimage today.

We begin to get an insight by remembering his primary scripture verse: "Thou shalt love the Lord thy God with all thy heart, and with all thy soul, and with all thy mind. This is the first and great commandment. And the second is like unto it. Thou shalt love thy neighbor as thyself. On these two commandments hang all the law and the prophets (Matt. 22:37-40)."[2] Wesley's devotional life was one means of fulfilling this goal. It became an avenue for him to more perfectly love God and others.

Certain key elements stand out in his devotional practices, which can help us as we seek to love God and others in the same way. *First, Wesley's devotional life has a realism about it.* When we study his devotional life, we sense we are following a fellow pilgrim in the faith. Wesley had ups and downs just like we do. His devotional life was not perfect just as ours is not. He made his share of mistakes as he went along.

One of the most graphic errors occurred around 1732. Wesley's devotions took a turn toward extreme self-examination. He became preoccupied with taking his spiritual pulse. At the back of his personal diary[3] he devised a system by which he could evaluate his progress, or lack of it. This was done by measuring his spiritual life against a set of predetermined questions. For each time Wesley failed to live up to a particular question, he put a dot on a chart. At the end of the week he totaled up the dots for each question in order to see how many times he had failed in that area. As we can plainly see, his system caused him to emphasize his faults. Wesley was practicing defeatist devotionalism!

This should be a warning to us. It is easy to slip into a devotional pattern which accentuates the negative. This is especially the case if we already have some problem with low self-esteem. We too easily practice the first half of

James 5:16, "Confess *your* faults to one another," but leave out the last half, "and pray for one another, *that you may be healed*" (RSV, *italics added*). As a result, our devotional life degenerates into spiritual neurosis.

Certainly we should not ignore the negative areas of our lives. We must continue to take failure and sin seriously. But Wesley's example does remind us that we find positive spiritual formation *not* by amplifying our problems but by applying God's grace. We can be thankful that Wesley corrected this mistake and abandoned the keeping of his "failure chart." We must also find a devotional style that accentuates the healing, restoring grace of God.

Wesley's devotional life has a realism about it. He did not have it all neatly worked out so that his devotional life hummed along for sixty years like a finely tuned automobile. He had to make adjustments along the way. At times he had to abandon some practices. He reminds us that we have to do the same thing in order to have a meaningful walk with the Lord.

Second, Wesley's devotional life has a discipline about it. The fact that he made some mistakes did not prevent him from continuing. He knew he had discovered the essential element in the Christian life, and he was determined to see it through. Wesley's resulting witness is remarkable. His daily diary entries indicate that for more than sixty years he faithfully practiced spiritual disciplines. To be sure, he varied the format and content from time to time. He was willing to experiment now and then. But his *basic intention* to relate to God personally did not waver.

Again, it is necessary to balance this long pattern of faithfulness with a note of realism. Wesley knew dry times just like we do. In fact, he had a symbol in his diary to record the fervency of his prayers. Many days show that his prayers were "cold" or "indifferent." But he kept at it knowing there would again be times of warmth and rejoicing.

I've heard more than one person say, "Well, I'm not getting much out of my devotions right now, so I'm going to eliminate them for a while until the warmth returns." While I can certainly empathize with these people, I have come to see that this approach can be spiritually devastating. It is in the dry times that we need to remain disciplined and faithful. In fact, true prayer grows out of a sense of the absence of God and our need of God.[4] If we give up in times of dryness and weakness, we will miss the joy of meeting the God who comes to us in our need. And we will fail to gain insight into the cause of the dryness. This will cause us to make the same mistakes again and again.[5]

Wesley addresses this issue and reminds us that we cannot base our devotional life on our emotions. We must center it in our will. It must flow out of our sense of need. We know what is right and we do it. We trust God to supply the appropriate emotions. Even in the absence of emotion we trust God to be at work in our lives. Discipline becomes the method by which our devotional life keeps going through fair weather and foul.

Third, Wesley's devotional life has a breadth about it. Beyond a doubt, he based his devotional life on the scriptures. He once remarked, "My ground is the Bible. Yea, I am a Bible-bigot. I follow it in all things, both great and small."[6] He continually referred to himself as homo unis libri—a man of one book. But by these words Wesley only revealed the touchstone and standard of his faith. He did not limit himself to the Bible. His scriptural foundation gave him a place to stand in his quest for spiritual life, but he was free to search for meaningful inspiration through a wide range of devotional material. Wesley knew the classics. He drew on Anglican, Puritan, Moravian, and Roman Catholic sources.[7] Consequently, his devotional life had a depth and variety which no single source could have provided. Using the Bible as his focus, Wesley was able to achieve a useful synthesis of spiritual input from these various sources.

Here is another important word for us. Too many in our time have limited themselves to a particular perspective in devotional content. More than that, some have settled for· a devotional life that is based in what I call "pop-spirituality." By that I mean it is trendy and grounded in the latest books from popular authors. There is a great need to discover the wealth of devotional material that spans the centuries of Christian history.[8] We stand on the shoulders of spiritual giants. Wesley challenges us to break out of a devotional narrowness and listen to the saints of the ages, all the while testing all things by the Bible.

Fourth, Wesley's devotional life has a community nature about it. He never allowed his spirituality to deteriorate into private religion. Whenever he could, Wesley shared insights with others. His diary is filled with references to his reading devotional works to others and discussing the implications. Wesley's letters are illustrative documents showing how he guided the spiritual progress of others.[9] In these ways he was not only ministering to the needs of others but also receiving help and inspiration from them as well.

Wesley's concern for corporate spirituality is most clearly seen in his formation of societies where people could find group support.[10] These groups became the hub for Methodism's life and growth. The late Bishop Gerald Ensley was correct when he observed that Wesley gathered believers through his preaching and nurtured them through the societies.[11]

It was through the societies that Wesley demonstrated the social dimension of spiritual formation. It was inconceivable to him that true devotion could ever remain individualized or internal. Authentic spirituality always thrust one into a community and the life of "social holiness." Wesley's prayers constantly reminded him that the world was his parish. His actions through the societies were the logical outworkings of genuine devotion and testimonies to the corporate nature of the devotional life.

Fifth, Wesley's devotional life has a church dimension about it. It is important for us to remember that Wesley never allowed his personal spirituality or the societies to become "substitute churches." He found his place in the regular worship of the Church of England, and he intended his followers to do the same. Wesley faithfully observed morning and evening prayers. He received the Lord's Supper an average of once every four or five days, usually at an Anglican altar.[12] And he kept the festival and fast days of the Anglican Church.[13]

Wesley did not do these things because he believed the Anglican Church was a "pure church" or that its principles and practices were beyond question. He did not remain an Anglican because everyone believed like he did. No, Wesley did it all for one reason—he knew that to be a Christian is to be a functioning member of the body of Christ. No one can be a Christian in isolation. Wesley's devotional life reminds us that there is no such thing as authentic spirituality apart from the church. God has called us to be in fellowship with the rest of the people of God. Our devotional life should motivate us toward that kind of body-life, not away from it.

In our day there is a renewed interest in spiritual formation and the devotional life. We are coming to see that we cannot meet the challenges of our age unless we are strengthened with inner resources. In the church we are coming to see that no amount of activity can substitute for a personal relationship with God through Jesus Christ. The example of John Wesley as a man of devotion is relevant for us as we look for insight and motivation in the spiritual life. The needs are as great now as then. God is as near now as then!

Questions for Discussion

1. Which of the qualities of Wesley's devotional life speaks most to you? Why?
2. What dangers do you see in some contemporary spiritual life movements?
3. Why is it necessary to have a scriptural foundation in a search for truth? What examples can you think of where a lack of scriptural foundation has led to problems?
4. How do you react to Wesley's staying in the Anglican Church despite its problems? What insight does this give about the nature of genuine renewal?

Chapter Two

Constant Company with Christ

WE TAKE a giant step forward in Christian devotion when we see it more as a life to be lived than as a time to be observed. Consequently, it is more appropriate to speak of a "devotional life" than a "devotional time." When we study Wesley's spirituality, we see this coming through loud and clear. He never divided his life into compartments. For him, the essence of life was spiritual. All of it could properly be called devotional.

In our time Henri Nouwen has expressed the same idea in these words: "If I cannot find God in the middle of my work—where my concerns and worries, pains, and joys are—it does not make sense to try to find him in the hours set free at the periphery of my life. If my spiritual life cannot grow and deepen in the midst of my ministry, how will it ever grow on the edges?"[1]

This is a good question for all of us to consider. Many have been brought up on the idea that devotions are the first moments of the morning and the last minutes of the evening. Devotional booklets are sometimes geared to telling us how to spend these *minutes* each day. While it is certainly appropriate to have a quiet time with God at the beginning and end of the day, we must not see that time as equal to the devotional life or separate from the rest of our day.

John Wesley sought for ways to express his spiritual life throughout the day. He found the way in what he called the "means of grace." These were spiritual disciplines which people used to express their faith and receive God's grace. They were divided into two categories: the instituted means of grace and the prudential means of grace.[2] The instituted means were those disciplines evident in the life and teaching of Jesus. The prudential means were those which had been developed by the church to give further order and expression to the Christian life. Taken together, they enabled a person to live a devotional life. The rest of the book will concentrate on examining these means of grace.

For Wesley, the chief instituted means of grace was prayer. It is not exaggerating to say that he lived to pray and prayed to live. He called prayer "the grand means of drawing near to God."[3] Prayer had this importance because Wesley understood the Christian faith as a life lived in relationship with God through Jesus Christ. Because this is so, prayer was the key to maintaining that relationship. It was the gift of God to humankind to facilitate and enrich the relationship. Furthermore, the absence of prayer was seen by Wesley to be the most common cause of spiritual dryness.[4] Nothing could substitute for prayer in maintaining the spiritual life.

Consequently, when we speak of the devotional life, we must begin with prayer. It is the "spiritual breathing" which sustains our life in Christ. It is the divine gift of communication and communion with our Creator. And when we turn to John Wesley, we gain many helpful insights which will improve our praying.

First of all, *Wesley prayed privately.* He believed that in private prayer one waited in quietness to receive the blessings of God.[5] Accordingly, he began his day in prayer. Much has been made about Wesley's habit of rising early, normally at 4:30 or 5:00 in the morning. While it is true that he did this for more than fifty years, it is also necessary to remember that he usually went to bed no later than 10:00. The principle lies not so much in the specific hour of rising as it does in the fact that Wesley directed his first thoughts toward God. He knew that to fix the mind on God early would create a divine consciousness that would remain with him throughout the day.

It is natural to ask how Wesley spent his times of private prayer. As we might expect, he was too methodical not to order his prayers in some way. He selected the common practice of having a weekly pattern, with each day devoted to a particular topic.[6] Written prayers formed the basis of his praying, but Wesley built into these prayers places for extemporaneous prayer.[7] The written prayers provided a focus for his praying and the extemporaneous prayers left room for spontaneity. In this way, Wesley felt he had the best of both worlds in his prayers.

This combination of prayers should still have an appeal to people today. In counseling others I have found that wandering thoughts are a nearly universal problem in prayer. Many have said something like this: "When I pray, I find my mind going off in a hundred directions. What can I do to keep it on track?" I often suggest using a combination of written and spontaneous prayers and praying with some sense of order and plan. The more focus we bring to prayer, the less troubled we will be with a wandering mind.

In our own day, Archbishop Anthony Bloom has given some good advice regarding written prayers. First, he states his belief that no one can sustain a *lifetime* of meaningful prayer without some use of written prayers.

But he goes on to urge that we never read a written prayer. Rather, we should *pray* it. This means that we actually get into the spirit of the prayer by reflecting on the words of the prayer, absorbing them, and then lifting them to God as the expressions of our own heart.[8] This has changed my whole outlook regarding written prayers. I now see they have never been intended for reading, but for *praying*.

Wesley also believed that by using written prayers we would enrich our understanding and expression of true prayer. By reflecting on the historic prayers of the church, we discover the format and main themes of prayer. We discover areas in our praying that are not receiving enough attention. We are helped to pray in a spirit of community with the church universal. So Wesley urged the early Methodists to let written prayers provide the base for prayer, with spontaneous prayers providing the freedom to respond to the special leadings of God from day to day.

Wesley's early morning prayers remind us of the importance of starting the day right. Norman Vincent Peale has rightly said, "To wake up creatively is an important skill. And it is a skill that can be cultivated."[9] Wesley cultivated the skill by having the mind of Christ formed within him at the start of the day.

But he did not stop there. Wesley prayed privately throughout the day. His diary indicates that he trained his mind to pray on the hour. These prayers were usually brief, sentence prayers of praise. They were Wesley's way of bringing the events of his life before God. After this "ejaculatory prayer," he normally spent the next five to seven minutes in meditation.

At this point it is easy to get the idea that Wesley's example is not realistic for those of us caught up in the hectic pace of modern living. But we must remember that

Wesley was no recluse. He did not live a monastic or detached life. On the contrary, he kept a schedule of work, writing, preaching, and traveling that is impressive even by today's standards. Obviously he did not withdraw each hour for devotional exercises. Instead, Wesley cultivated the habit *internally*. He learned to be fully engaged in the affairs of life and simultaneously involved in prayer to God. Wesley had trained himself to turn his "inner voice" to the Creator.

This is the true meaning of Paul's exhortation to pray without ceasing. Wesley called it "the breath of our spiritual life" and suggested a person could no more cease to pray than cease to breathe.[10] Admittedly, this kind of praying does not come easily and not without struggle and gaps. But even modern writers like Thomas Kelly in his *Testament of Devotion* continue to challenge us to this dimension of devotional life.

For some, unceasing prayer is developed through the use of creative reminders. I know persons who tape a prayer reminder to their telephone. Each time it rings, they pray for the person on the other end of the line. Business executives write in a midday appointment with God and thereby bring their faith directly into their work. Others place prayer reminders throughout the house. As they see them, they pray. Some persons set their digital watches to beep on the hour and use that as a call to prayer. Each of these people is exemplifying Wesley's concern to pray throughout the day.

Wesley also prayed privately at the end of the day. This experience gave him a sense of closure and commitment in his spiritual life. The focus for each of his evening prayers was again written, with room for spontaneity. Wesley reviewed the day and made appropriate confession for sins committed. He made resolutions by which he sought to amend his life. And he committed himself to the care and protection of God as he went to sleep. Wesley remarked that by doing this, he was able to sleep in peace nearly all the days of his life.

We need to learn the art of going to sleep correctly. Too often I find myself working right up to the time to go to bed. Consequently, when I get into bed, my mind is still whirling. Subconsciously I continue working rather than resting. The next day I awaken with a sense of fatigue rather than rejuvenation. I find I am not alone in this. Wesley reminds us that we need a time to unwind and commit the day and ourselves to God. Private prayer at the end of the day is one way of "turning loose" so we can go to sleep with the burdens of the day laid aside.

Wesley prayed privately, and by doing so, he framed his day and made every moment a potential "God-moment." But he did not stop with private prayer. He also *prayed corporately*. Wesley knew that private prayer alone is not sufficient for a healthy spiritual life, so he consciously looked for ways to pray with others.

The most natural way to do this was via the *Book of Common Prayer*. As a faithful Anglican, Wesley joined daily with others in the services of morning and evening prayer. Sometimes the group numbered only a handful; at other times he might be in a parish church or cathedral. But always Wesley was consistent in his practice of corporate prayer.

It is unfortunate that denominations in the Wesleyan tradition do not have a counterpart to morning and evening prayer. One of the highlights of my stay at Wesley's Chapel was our use of the Daily Office. The group was usually small, but the observance of corporate prayer reminded us of the church as the community of faith and prayer as the focal point for living. When we do not have regular opportunities to pray corporately, it is possible for the spiritual life to become excessively private.

Increasing segments of the charismatic movement and other groups involved in church renewal are rediscovering the vitality of corporate prayer. Here in America numbers of groups meet for prayer and the celebration of the Lord's Supper. In Korea, multitudes gather for prayer each day before going to work. The result is a deepening of koinonia and an outpouring of the power of God. Examples like these help to confirm Wesley's conviction that God does nothing except in answer to prayer.

We can be sure that Wesley would encourage us to find times to regularly pray with others. It might be an ongoing prayer group or with only one prayer partner. A prayer-chain ministry is another possibility. But regardless of format, a commitment to corporate prayer reflects the Wesleyan spirit. It bears witness to the fact that we are members of the larger Body of Christ.

To know that Wesley prayed privately and corporately does not exhaust the richness of his prayer life. So a few miscellaneous comments are in order. For one thing, we naturally want to know how Wesley prayed. Several factors shed light on this subject. First, he varied the form of his prayers. Having already shown that written prayers were at the heart of his praying, it is now important to note that Wesley used prayers from a variety of sources: *The Book of Common Prayer,* his own prayer manual,[11] other prayer books of the time, and prayers from the early church. To these Wesley added his own extemporaneous prayers. His main concern was to communicate meaningfully with God. He varied his prayers to avoid getting into a rut.

Second, Wesley prayed audibly and meditatively. He prayed aloud, alone and in groups. His diary shows that he often enjoyed combining verbal prayer with hymn singing. But Wesley also knew the value of silence. Again, his diary reveals that much of his praying was done via the inner voice. Mental prayer allowed him the freedom to pray at all times and in a variety of circumstances. This was the secret to Wesley's hourly devotions, and it is a reminder to us that we need an interior holy of holies for our spiritual pilgrimage.

Third, Wesley expressed the full range of prayer. He praised, confessed, gave thanks, interceded for others, and let his own requests be made known unto God. Through such prayers, Wesley expressed the full range of emotions: joy, sorrow, compassion, concern, trust. One of the most striking features of his praying was honesty. Often Wesley bared his soul before God in doubts, questions, and even cries of anguish. When he was undergoing trials in Georgia, especially in his relation to Sophie Hopkey, Wesley recorded that he tried to pray but could not. In that moment God seemed beyond reach, and he did not try to cover up the feeling with pious, artificial words. Consequently, Wesley's prayers have the ring of reality. When he prays with warmth and affection, we can know he is being genuine. When he records that his prayers were cold or indifferent, we can identify with him. In both dimensions we have a realistic guide.

Fourth, Wesley read, studied, and used the prayers of others. He made a practice of collecting prayers from others. By this he meant that he either copied in full or abbreviated the prayer of another Christian. Some of the others were well-known persons like Jeremy Taylor or William Law. Others were little-known colleagues. But regardless of the source, Wesley used insights from others' prayers to advance his own spiritual life. When people came to him seeking help in their prayer life, Wesley often shared these prayers with them. This fact largely explains why Wesley's first publication was *A Collection of Forms of Prayer for Every Day in the Week* (1733). These prayers, which also reflected Wesley's weekly devotional pattern, helped to guide others in their praying.

Here is another important principle for us today. We need to get in touch with the devotional classics. When we do so, we find we are not alone in our spiritual pilgrimage. Others have shared similar victories and defeats. They have asked our questions, felt our pains, and experienced our blessings. They are lights for our pathway, aids for our journey.

It is not easy to bring this chapter to a close. Examining Wesley's prayer life generates a lot of momentum. And even this treatment has barely scratched the surface. Perhaps what Wesley would want most out of our study is for us to come away with the conviction that *God can be known*. In the words of the hymnwriter, we really can "walk with him and talk with him." Wesley would not want us to examine his prayer life as an end in itself. He never put his spirituality on display. In fact, Wesley developed a code so the casual observer would not be able to break in upon the experience. The only reason for looking at Wesley's prayer example is that we will "go and do likewise."

Questions for Discussion

1. Would you say that your devotional life has been on the edges of your life or in the midst of it? Why?
2. Share the ways you have discovered to direct the first thoughts of your day to God.
3. How do you respond to the idea of a weekly cycle in your prayers? How might this help make your prayer list more manageable?
4. Do you use any prayer reminders to help bring more of your day to God?
5. How do you end your day devotionally?

Chapter Three

The All-Sufficient Word

THE SPIRITUAL LIFE must have an objective base. Private revelations must be scrutinized against a recognized and established norm. To put it in biblical language, we must "test the spirits to see whether they are of God" (1 John 4:1, RSV). Failure to do this occasionally results in tragic stories and bizarre acts. Our generation will long remember the Jonestown incident as a classic example of misguided, even maniacal spiritualism.

John Wesley knew that an objective standard was necessary for genuine spirituality. For him, that standard was the Bible. He was committed to the centrality and authority of scripture. Although Wesley read hundreds of books on a wide range of subjects, he continually referred to himself as *homo unis libri*—a man of one book. Even though he published approximately six hundred works on various themes, he resolutely maintained that he allowed no rule, whether of faith or practice, other than the Holy Scriptures.[1] In the preface to his *Standard Sermons* Wesley exclaims, "O give me that book! At any price, give me the book of God! . . . here is knowledge enough for me."[2]

Wesley confirmed this exclamation with an amazing example of faithfulness to the study of the Bible. For sixty-five years the Bible was his daily companion in the life of faith. It was his primary guide for living the holy life. As the heirs of Wesley, we need to make a clear affirmation of the authority of scripture, not as one source among several, but as *the* norm for Christian thought and conduct. We need to declare that the Bible is *the* standard by which the results of tradition, reason, and experience are checked.[3]

At the same time it is important for us to remember that, for Wesley, the primary value of scripture was not its serving as some sort of cold, objective standard. Rather, he saw the primary value of the Bible in its unique ability to bring men and women into an encounter with Almighty God. Therefore, we may say that the primary value of scripture (rightly understood) is *devotional.*

That being the case, we must ask, "How did Wesley use the Bible to cultivate devotional life?" And further, "How can we use his example to guide us in the devotional use of scripture today?" In response to these questions a number of principles stand out.

First, Wesley read the Bible worshipfully. By that we mean that he read the Bible in an unhurried, reverent manner. He wrote about this and said, "Here then I am, far from the busy ways of men. I sit down alone: only God is here. In his presence I open, I read his book; for this end, to find the way to heaven."[4]

To insure that his Bible study times were unhurried, Wesley chose the early hours of the morning and the quiet hours of the evening. These times allowed him the space to meditate on what he read. His main goal was quality, not quantity. It is true that Wesley normally read a chapter per sitting, but sometimes he would read only a few verses. His desire was to encounter God, and when he did that, the amount he read was not the most important thing. In this regard, Wesley reminds us that we cannot meaningfully read the Bible on the run. To be alone with God and God's word requires a time all its own and a corresponding attitude of reverence and attention.

Second, Wesley read the Bible systematically. His usual practice was to follow the table of daily readings in the *Book of Common Prayer.* By using these, he was able to read through the Old Testament once per year and the New Testament several times. This approach also allowed Wesley to read contextually rather than haphazardly. Wesley believed that Christians should know "the whole counsel of God." He exemplified this by reading the Old and New Testaments as well as the Apocrypha.

It would be wrong, however, to suppose that Wesley was only looking for experience when he read the Bible devotionally. He also wanted to *know* the word of God. He saw no dichotomy between scholarly study of the Bible and reading for spiritual enrichment. Any new information or insight was further inspiration from God, and he received it as such. Wesley also brought to the reading of scripture a knowledge of the original languages and the best study aids of his day.

Wesley demonstrated his concern for biblical knowledge by preparing the *Explanatory Notes* for the Old and New Testaments.[5] These notes were largely drawn from the writings of others, but they represent Wesley's views on the selected texts. He said that he prepared the notes for "plain, unlettered men . . . who . . . reverence and love the Word of God, and have a desire to save their souls."[6] Consequently, the comments are generally devoid of technical, scholarly terminology. But even a casual reading of them shows them to be substantive and beneficial.

Wesley challenges us at the point of systematic reading. Important questions emerge: "Am I reading the Bible in a way that brings me in contact with the whole of it?" "Do I read scripture in large enough portions to see isolated passages in their larger context?" "Do I use responsible aids to add the insights of others to my own study of God's word?" "Do I have any means of marking, noting, and recording my discoveries?" In all these ways we are being true to Wesley's example which reminds us that an in-depth knowledge of scripture requires a systematic approach.

Third, Wesley read the Bible comprehensively. He knew that he had a lifetime to read the Bible, so he did not have to hurry. Nor did he have to be content with a shallow or surface reading. In typical Wesley fashion, he developed a method which provided a comprehensive experience. The main elements of the method are as follows:

1. Dailiness—morning and evening;
2. Singleness of purpose—to know God's will;
3. Correlation—to compare scripture with scripture;
4. Prayerfulness—to receive instruction from the Holy Spirit;
5. Resolution—to put into practice what is learned.[7]

This last point leads us to another important principle in Wesley's devotional use of the Bible: he read it purposefully. He wrote, "Whatever light you receive, should be used to the uttermost, and that immediately."[8] For Wesley, this meant at least two things. First, it meant the personal application of God's word to our lives. Second, it meant that we should seek to teach others what we have learned.

Related to personal application, Wesley encouraged people to pause frequently and examine themselves by what they were reading. We would call this reflective reading. He said that by doing this we would find the Bible "to be indeed the power of God unto present and eternal salvation."[9] This discovery would move us to form appropriate resolutions about the way we will live from day to day.

In our own day, Paul Little has captured this same commitment to application through a series of questions:

1. Is there an example for me to follow?
2. Is there a sin for me to avoid?
3. Is there a command for me to obey?
4. Is there a promise for me to claim?
5. What does this passage teach me about God or Jesus Christ?
6. Is there a difficulty for me to explore?
7. Is there something in this passage I should pray about today?[10]

Wesley would endorse these kinds of questions for all of us as we study the Bible. He would want to know that our time in God's word is changing us and bringing our lives into greater conformity to the image of Christ. He would echo the words of the psalmist, "I hasten and do not delay to keep thy commandments" (119:60, RSV).

But purposefulness is never made private. Full application means that we seek to teach others what we have learned. Wesley put it plainly, "What I thus learn, that I teach."[11] This principle is confirmed many times over in his diary where we see Wesley sharing insights with others as he visited with them. Sometimes this took the form of more formal readings from scripture and other devotional material. At other times, Wesley passed along insights in casual conversation. But always he was open to ways and means of helping others grow in their faith.

A word of caution is in order at this point. Nowhere does Wesley appear to be pushy or dogmatic in his sharing with others. He did not try to make universal his experience and force it on others. Rather, his approach was more sensitive. He seems to have allowed the experience of another to be a doorway through which he could share what God had taught him in a similar experience. This approach is in contrast to some today who have a word from the Lord for us which must be forthrightly obeyed or our spirituality is called into question. Wesley never operated that way. Rather, he shared the insights he had gained humbly, knowing that if it were truly a word from the Lord for that person, the Holy Spirit would make the application in that person's life.

It is important to see that Wesley's willingness to teach others what he had learned from scripture was based on his belief in the multifaceted usefulness of the Bible. In the explanatory note for Second Timothy 3:16, he said that scripture is *"profitable for doctrine, for instruction of the ignorant, for the reproof or conviction of them that are in error or sin, for the correction or amendment of whatever is amiss, and for instructing or training up the children of God in all righteousness."*[12] With such a broad relevance, it is not surprising that Wesley found many occasions to pass along insights to others. And still today our faith takes on a new dimension when we can relate the events of our lives to the teachings of scripture.

What we have said thus far has dealt primarily with Wesley's use of scripture as an individual. There is a final point which completes the picture. *Wesley read and used the Bible corporately.* He knew there was value for the community of faith to sit under God's word. So in the *General Rules* Wesley required the early Methodists to be faithful in attending services where the word of God was preached and taught. This meant both the Anglican services at the parish churches and the various meetings connected with the early Methodist movement: bands, classes, societies, and preaching services. It also meant faithfulness in the reading and explanation of scripture in family devotions.[13]

As the Methodist movement grew, Wesley brought his preachers together for annual conferences. At these meetings they sought solutions to problems which they faced. Their answers, recorded in the *Conference Minutes,* are salted with references to scripture.[14] It is clear that in matters of church administration Wesley sought the guidance of the Bible.

In the corporate dimension there is perhaps no place where the influence of scripture shines through more than in Wesleyan hymnody. It is true that the early Methodists sang their faith. It is also true that virtually every line in the hymns had a scriptural basis.[15] Some of the allusions are unmistakable; others are subtle, revealing the minute and comprehensive knowledge of scripture the Wesleys had. All of the hymns help to confirm the fact that the early Methodists sought every way possible to digest inwardly the biblical message. We may be sure that Wesley would encourage the use of the Bible in corporate ways. He would delight in seeing small groups meeting weekly to study the Bible. He would urge the general church to conduct its business with this question as its guiding star: "What saith the scriptures?" And I dare to believe that this kind of attention to the Bible would achieve for us, even as it did for Wesley and early Methodism, a foundation and a guiding light for spirituality and ministry in the world.

The devotional use of scripture recognizes and affirms the comprehensiveness of the Bible. There is no area where the message of scripture is not relevant. But it can only do its work in those who know it and who come to it worshipfully, systematically, comprehensively, purposefully, and corporately. At the heart of it, when we read the Bible, we are really asking two questions: "Do I expect to meet God?" and, "Am I willing to obey God?"[16] John Wesley would want to know how his spiritual children answer both questions.

Questions for Discussion

1. Why is it important to have an objective basis for faith? What dangers or excesses have you observed when such a basis has been absent?
2. Share methods or materials you have been using in reading the Bible. What kinds of approaches minister to you most in your use of scripture?
3. What needs do you feel right now in the area of Bible study? Perhaps someone in the discussion group will have a suggestion to help you meet that need.
4. Discuss the ways you seek to apply what you learn from Bible reading. How does scripture come alive in your daily living?

Chapter Four

Food for the Journey

TRUE SPIRITUALITY always exists in relation to the church. As we have seen, even prayer and Bible study have their corporate expressions in Wesleyan devotional life. This truth is continued and highlighted in the third means of grace, the Lord's Supper. Albert Outler has rightly commented that Wesley believed the Lord's Supper to be "literally indispensable in the Christian life."[1] Wesley's diary shows that he backed up that conviction by communing on the average of once every four or five days. In our current examination of Wesleyan devotion, we cannot fail to grasp the significance of this dimension of spirituality.

Over the last fifteen years of my ministry, experience has shown me that many in the Wesleyan tradition are basically ignorant of the nature and importance of the Lord's Supper in the Christian life. There is a revival of sacramental awareness and theology taking place in the church today, but large numbers are yet to be touched by this wave of renewal. Consequently, many people absent themselves all too frequently from the Lord's table, and they do so with only vague notions as to why.

For the concerns of this study it is not too elementary to ask, "What is the sacrament of the Lord's Supper?" "What are we participating in when we kneel to receive the juice and bread?" When confronted by this question in his day, Wesley provided a threefold answer.[2] First, he said that the Communion is a *memorial meal*. When we eat the bread and drink from the cup, our minds are directed back to the once-for-all act of redemption wrought on our behalf by Christ himself. Like many other Christians before and after him, Wesley understood the juice and bread to be symbols of the New Covenant and reminders that this covenant is still in force.

But (and this is very important), his understanding of "memorial" did not stop with this. Looking to Jesus' own words, "Do this in *remembrance* of me" (Luke 22:19, RSV, *italics added*) he emphasized the Hebraic understanding of remembering. Truly to remember something or someone meant more than recollection. It meant to recall an event so thoroughly that the event comes alive, anew and afresh in the present. For Wesley, it was this sense of remembering that should characterize our reception of the Lord's Supper. We should remember Christ and our experience of him in such a way that we leave the table serving the risen Savior!

This being the case, Wesley could speak of a second dimension in the Lord's Supper, *the real presence of Christ*. At this point many enter a new phase of understanding Wesley's sacramental theology. Most members of the church have an awareness of memorial, but real presence is another matter. Therefore, it is important for us to know what Wesley meant. We are helped by knowing two things he did not mean. First, he did not mean transubstantiation. He did not believe there is any material change in the elements themselves whereby they become the body and blood of Christ.

Second, Wesley did not mean consubstantiation. This view held that while the bread and wine are not changed in their composition, Christ is nevertheless present *in* the elements which are received. This position was held by those who could not subscribe to transubstantiation, but who nevertheless wanted to keep the presence of Christ localized in the elements themselves.

Wesley preferred the position of the Anglicanism of his day, i.e., real presence. This simply means that by his own choice the risen Christ is truly present whenever the Lord's Supper is observed. Christ does not come through the bread and cup; he comes through the Spirit. But Christ is *really* there.

This being so, it is easy to see why Wesley saw the Lord's Supper as a powerful means of grace. And because Wesley could never limit the activity of grace, he saw the Lord's Supper as communicating prevenient, justifying, or sanctifying grace.[3] He understood the primary value of Communion to be for those who were already Christian, but experience taught him that some had actually become Christians while participating in the sacrament. He wrote, "Ye are the witnesses. For many now present now know, the very beginning of your conversion to God . . . was wrought at the Lord's Supper."[4]

This explains why Methodists have always practiced open Communion. The invitation to partake of the sacrament is made to anyone who truly and earnestly repents of sin,[5] not to those who are members of this or that particular church. Albert Outler is right when he describes Wesley's view in these words: "It is always *God's* grace, it is never at man's disposal. Thus, it cannot be sequestered by any sacerdotal authority."[6]

Lest Wesley's openness at this point be confused with indifference, it should be remembered that he put great emphasis upon preparing to receive the Lord's Supper. This will be discussed later in the chapter, but it is important to mention it here. Wesley's openness was based on an understanding of the comprehensiveness of God's grace. Grace is offered in the sacrament, and it can accomplish whatever God purposes for the one who receives it.

The third dimension of the Lord's Supper for Wesley was its serving as *a pledge*. By *pledge* Wesley meant a promise of the future glory which awaits the Christian in heaven. The presence of the sacrament in the church now is an assurance to Christians that the heavenly banquet awaits us after death. In this same regard Wesley also saw our reception of the elements as one tangible contact with the great cloud of witnesses who have preceded us. In short, this dimension of Communion makes it a celebration meal as we praise God for the reality of everlasting life and anticipate our entrance into heaven.

With this threefold view of the Lord's Supper before us, it is hardly surprising that Wesley made it a vital part of the devotional life. True spirituality includes the elements of contemplation, experience, and hope. Each of these is realized through Communion. As we remember Christ, we are able to contemplate the depth and vitality of Christ's sacrifice for us and our commitment to him. As a means of grace, we experience the presence of Christ asking that he meet us at the point of our need with forgiveness, healing, power, etc. And finally, as a pledge, we partake as children of promise and hope. We hold in our hands and take into our bodies the physical dimension of God's promise to receive us to himself.

The significance of all this in Wesleyan spirituality can be described using Wesley's own words: "Let every one, therefore, who has either any desire to please God, or any love of his own soul, obey God, and consult the good of his own soul, by communicating every time he can."[7]

The early Methodist movement became a living testimony to Wesley's concern. Methodist preaching services were forbidden to conflict with sacramental services in the Anglican Church. Many times Wesley personally led the Methodists to the parish church to receive the Lord's Supper. As Anglican priests began to deny the sacrament to Methodists, Wesley used his own prerogatives as an Anglican clergyman to devise ways for his followers to have the sacrament. And as a last resort, he even allowed Communion to be served in Methodist gatherings. In the Christian pilgrimage, he did not want his people to lack the food for the journey.

As we think about the place of the Lord's Supper in our spiritual formation, we can easily be moved to acts of rededication to participate in this central act of worship. Wesley would rejoice in this and urge all of us to a new appreciation of the sacrament. At the same time, he would know that any attention to Communion brings with it certain practical questions and concerns. It was so in his day, and is still so today. In the final section of this chapter, I want to address a number of these concerns. Not to do so robs us of a full measure of devotion to this aspect of the spiritual life.

In Wesley's day, and to a large extent in ours, no problem perplexes more people than "eating and drinking in an unworthy manner." Misunderstanding this phrase has caused people to refrain from receiving the Lord's Supper lest they eat and drink damnation upon themselves. Consequently, the Lord's Supper is not an integral part of their spiritual formation. Ironically, Wesley himself dealt more extensively with this issue than the others we will examine. His insights remain highly instructive.

Basically, Wesley felt that confusion reigned because of a misreading of Paul's statement in First Corinthians

11:27-29. In his day, as now, people tended to read the verse and wrongly assume, "I should not eat *because I may be unworthy.*" In other words, they put the problem in their person and character. Wesley responded,

> Here is not a word said of being unworthy to eat and drink. Indeed, he does speak of eating and drinking *unworthily;* but that is quite a different thing; so he has told us himself. In this very chapter we are told that by eating and drinking unworthily is meant, taking the holy Sacrament in such a rude and disorderly way, that one was "hungry, and another drunken." But what is that to *you?* Is there any danger of *your* doing so,—of your eating and drinking *thus unworthily?*[8]

This radically shifts the meaning of the problem. It puts it in the *manner* of communing, not the character of the communicant. Wesley goes on to point out that if we abstain from Communion because of a sense of unworthiness due to our sinfulness, then everyone would abstain! We are all sinners saved by grace. In fact, the Lord's Supper (as a means of grace) is designed for sinners! It is not an offer to those who think themselves to be sinless. For Wesley, the only problem was to approach the Lord's Table without a repentant heart.[9] The only person who could ever stand before God in a worthy manner was our Lord. Everyone, before and since, has been "unworthy." That is precisely who the invitation is for, in order that God's grace may abound!

If that were not enough to persuade the hesitant, Wesley added another dimension. He reminded his followers that the invitation to Communion was in the form of command: "*Do this* in remembrance of me" (*italics added*). He pointed out that any Christian desires to obey the commandments of God.[10] In Wesley's eyes we come much closer to defiling ourselves by willfully disobeying a command of Christ than we ever would by running the risk of unworthy character. The call to Communion is a call to obedience more than it is a call to moral perfection.

A personal word is in order at this point. In my ministry, I have discovered that these two points from Wesley himself are often sufficient to bring absent persons back to the Lord's Supper. We need to share these ideas with those today who may have wrongly excluded themselves from this important means of grace. If as a reader you are among those who have done so, I would urge you to reflect on what Wesley has said and find yourself at the Communion table at the next opportunity.

The second problem regarding Communion is related to the first. It is the problem of preparation. If we do not have to have attained any particular state of righteousness, then what do we have to do? Here Wesley gives an answer that is both challenging and gracious. The challenge, as we have seen, is to come to Communion with a repentant heart. This eliminates any idea that Wesley would condone an uncritical ritual which simply herds people to the altar. He would leave open the possibility that we would not go to Communion on certain occasions. These occasions would *not* be because we felt sinful; but rather, because we were unwilling to repent of our sin. If we stubbornly refuse to respond to God's convicting grace, and we choose to continue in known sin, then we would do well to refrain. But again, those times (if we are Christian) would be extremely rare.

Practically speaking, this preparation should take place through self-examination and prayer and (when possible) even a day or two in advance of Communion. Wesley often used his Thursday evening devotions to mark the beginning of his preparation for Sunday's Communion. But Wesley knew that this kind of advanced preparation was not always possible, so he wrote that this was not "absolutely necessary."[11] In another place he showed "that no fitness is required at the time of communicating, but a sense of our state, of our utter sinfulness and helplessness."[12] Consequently, we find that Communion services in the Anglican and Methodist traditions allowed time in the service for would-be communicants to cultivate this kind of attitude. In our day, we should find ways to prepare our hearts, that we might come to God openly and humbly. In coming that way we are more likely to receive the benefits of God's grace.

The third practical problem has to do with the frequency of offering and receiving the sacrament. The rubric for the Order of Communion in the *Book of Common Prayer* (1662) stated that "in cathedral and collegiate churches and college, where there are many priests and deacons, they shall *all receive the Communion with the priest every Sunday at the least.*"[13] As with some of our rules today, this particular regulation was being largely ignored. The result was that many only received the Communion twice a year, some only quarterly, and others perhaps once a month.

Wesley was crystal clear as to his position, writing that "no man can have any pretence to Christian piety, who does not receive it (not once a month, but) as often as he can."[14] In a sermon he preached in 1788 wherein he reflected on the past fifty years of Methodism, Wesley showed that Communion was an established part of the Sunday service.[15] And taking it one step farther, it is important to note that in Wesley's instructions to the infant American church, he urged the elders "to administer the Supper of the Lord on every Lord's Day."[16]

Here again, many of us find ourselves brought to reflection by Wesley's words. While it is true that we do not (and should not) have to legalistically follow every detail in Wesley's writings, neither should we be casually unconcerned when we do not follow him. Our practices should at least reflect Wesley's *spirit*. And we have to admit that the failure of many churches to have frequent Communion is based on motives other than those of which Wesley would approve. We should be grateful that contemporary resources like Hoyt Hickman's *Word & Table* are reminding us of the importance of the sacrament of the Lord's Supper. And regardless of the specific practice adopted, we should strive to reflect the significance which Communion has in our tradition.

In some places this will mean an intentional educating of the congregation, drawing on the kinds of ideas that have been shared in this chapter. In some cases it may mean standing against prevailing opinions to have Communion as rarely as possible. Increasingly it may be that churches will find ways to offer weekly Communion to their people, thus reviving the frequent offering of this means of grace to those who desire it.

It is in this the context of an offered sacrament that we can raise the final practical problem, i.e., who should receive it? By what has already been said, the question is answered in terms of open and closed Communion, and it is answered in terms of any supposed requirement of spiritual attainment. At this point, I am writing more to deal with the question of children's participation in the sacrament. This is a practical question which parents have often asked.

For Wesley, the indispensable prerequisite for receiving Communion was baptism. As an Anglican priest, he upheld the church's requirement that one should receive

Communion only after confirmation, usually between the ages of fourteen and sixteen. However, because Wesley had some personal doubts about the value of confirmation, he was willing to allow for some exceptions if children evidenced a special maturity and desire regarding the sacrament. His own example was a case in point. His father, Samuel, felt John was especially spiritually sensitive at age nine, and allowed him to be confirmed and receive Communion at that age. Consequently, he made proven spiritual sensitivity, not the touch of a bishop's hands in confirmation, the bottom line for coming to the Lord's Table. This, however, should not obscure the fact that in actual practice Wesley largely followed the church in administering the Lord's Supper to those who had been confirmed.[17]

Admittedly, this leaves us with something of an option. As parents, we may follow the church and postpone our children's first Communion until after confirmation. But if our children have been baptized, we may follow the lesser-traveled way of spiritual sensitivity and allow them to receive the sacrament somewhat earlier. If we choose to allow our children to partake before confirmation, then at the very least we should instruct them in the significance of what they are doing and sense that they have an appropriate appreciation and reverence for the event.

I hope this chapter has been enlightening as we have considered the importance of the Lord's Supper in the devotional life. As professing Christians, we may confidently approach the sacrament knowing that Christ himself will mediate grace in relation to our needs. And knowing that, we may indeed find ourselves greatly blessed as we receive the bread and juice into ourselves.

Questions for Discussion

1. Which aspect of the nature of the Lord's Supper means the most to you?
2. Have you ever struggled over the issue of unworthiness in receiving Communion? Do you know someone who has? How are Wesley's comments helpful?
3. Discuss the place and significance of Communion in your life in the past. What new insights or motivations did this chapter provide to make it more meaningful in the future?

Chapter Five

Hunger for Righteousness

IN THE HISTORY of Christian spirituality, the theme of self-denial is of major importance. Saints of the ages have recognized that the spiritual life is not only concerned with what we receive, but also with what we give up. It is this rhythm of giving and receiving which brings balance to our faith.

In the Wesleyan tradition, particularly in terms of the means of grace, the element of self-denial is most visible in the discipline of fasting. It is significant that Wesley included it among the five instituted means of grace. He was persuaded that fasting was "fully established in the church of God" and practiced by Christ himself (Matt. 6:16).[1] That was sufficient to warrant its use in the present.

Wesley's advocacy of fasting was not without the knowledge that it had been abused across the centuries, often expressing itself in bizarre fashion. He wrote, "Of all the means of grace there is scarce any concerning which men have run into greater extremes, than that of...religious fasting."[2] His own life, particularly during the Holy Club and Georgia periods, was a case in point. But extremes notwithstanding, Wesley believed the practice of fasting was a definite aid in spiritual growth.

As we approach the subject, it will be most helpful if we examine some of the main features of a Wesleyan theology of fasting. From there we can move to examine Wesley's own practices and those of the early Methodists. Based on this, we will be in a position to formulate our use of the discipline for spiritual formation.

Wesley's most systematic treatment of fasting comes in his seventh discourse on the Sermon on the Mount. This sermon was included in the *Standard Sermons,* which gives further doctrinal significance to what is said therein. We will be on safest ground if we simply attempt to grasp the ideas Wesley presents in this message.

He recognized the fundamental definition for fasting in the Bible: to abstain from food. He also knew that the Bible carried examples of additional practices which accompanied fasting, but which had no necessary connection with it. These Wesley called "indifferent circumstances."[3] His main concern was to advocate fasting as a discipline standing alone and without additional trappings.

Wesley was aware that the times for fasting varied widely in scripture, going all the way up to forty days and forty nights. But he believed the most common practice to be for one day, from morning until evening. He not only found scriptural support for this, but also evidence that this was the usual manner of the early church. Wesley knew that Wednesday and Friday were widely reserved for fasting by early Christians, to which were added other stated fast days throughout the year.[4]

Biblically, Wesley was willing to recognize several types of fasting. The most common was not eating any *food* at all during the prescribed fast. It is important to note that Wesley left open the use of some liquid during the period, although he knew there might be times when a person would not eat or drink anything. The second type was abstinence, which he felt could be used when one could not fast entirely. A sick person might choose this form. Interestingly, Wesley could not find an example of this kind of fasting in the Bible, but he wrote "neither can I condemn it; for the scripture does not. It may have a use and receive a blessing from God."[5] The third type was abstaining from pleasant food. This kind of fast was used in scripture by those who did not want to defile themselves with sumptuous fare.

An important principle emerges at this point. Wesley made a conscious break with a portion of the Christian tradition which had emphasized the side of bodily mortification in fasting. He was sternly against any use of fasting which sought to prove spirituality by extremes in physical asceticism. He wrote, "Yea, the body may sometimes be afflicted too much, so as to be unfit for the works of our calling. This also we are to diligently guard against; for we ought to preserve our health as a good gift of God."[6]

The sum of all is this: when one approached fasting sanely and with the biblical perspective, it could be a beneficial discipline. It could be well used by those who were under conviction, by those who were aware of intemperance in food and drink, and by those who wanted to find additional and special times for prayer.[7] In fact, it was the connection between prayer and fasting which Wesley most wanted to emphasize in the devotional life. This is why believers could devote themselves to regular fast days, not waiting for a spiritual crisis to lead them to fasting.

In the practice of any spiritual discipline, we are helped by the example of others, even though we do not have to feel compelled to follow them in every detail. In the practice of fasting, Wesley's example is of help in providing a balanced approach. For the most part, he

followed the custom of the Anglican Church which encouraged fasting on Fridays, during the forty days of Lent,
the four Ember days, and the three Rogation days.[8] Between 1725 and 1738, when Wesley was consciously
patterning his practices after the early church, he observed
the Wednesday and Friday fast days. After 1738, however,
he seems to have returned to the weekly observance on
Friday. In short, Wesley was a good churchman and
exhorted the early Methodists to be the same.

Using Friday as an example, we can reconstruct the
main features of Wesley's period of fasting. He began his
fast following the evening meal on Thursday. Usually he
did not eat again until Friday afternoon when he broke
fast with tea. But as we have seen, Wesley would take
some liquid during the fast (water, tea, or broth) if he felt
it was necessary for his health. The main thing was that
the time was especially devoted to prayer. The overall
purpose was that

> it be done unto the Lord, with our eye singly
> fixed on Him. Let our intention herein be this, and
> this alone, to glorify our Father which is in heaven;
> to express our sorrow and shame for our manifold
> transgressions of his holy law; to wait for an increase
> of purifying grace, drawing our affections to things
> above; to add seriousness and earnestness to our
> prayers; to avert the wrath of God, and to obtain all
> the great and precious promises which he hath made
> to us Jesus Christ.[9]

Using the principle that what he learned he taught,
Wesley encouraged the early Methodists to include fasting
in their spiritual formation. In the *General Rules* of 1743,
Wesley encouraged the United Societies to practice fasting
as one example of "attending upon all the ordinances of

God."[10] In the *General Rules* Wesley laid down no specific injunctions as to the time, frequency, or duration of the fast. But very early in the movement, Friday came to be the Methodist fast day.

In 1744, when Wesley held the first annual conference, he addressed the subject of fasting. He wrote, "[God] led all of you to it, when you first set out. How often do you fast now? Every Friday? In what degree? I purpose generally to eat only vegetables on Friday, and to take only toast and water in the mornings."[11] At this time in his life we can see that Wesley was practicing abstinence more than total fasting and recommending the same to his preachers at the conference. The avoidance of rigorous asceticism and the primacy of prayer and devotion continue to characterize the spirit of Methodist fasting.

In 1768, Wesley issued a directive to the societies fixing quarterly fast days in September, January, April, and July. Additionally, the annual conference checked up further on the practice of Friday fasting. Interestingly, the subject of fasting led into a discussion of Christian perfection, showing that in the pursuit of holiness the issue of self-denial was significant.[12] Wesley also continued to view fasting as an act which God often chose to bless with revival among the people.[13]

When we inquire as to the feelings of the early Methodists about fasting, the attitude of Hannah Ball is typical. She wrote that the weekly fast day was "a fast-day to my body, but a feast day to my soul." In the same record she went on to speak of this as a time of "unusual freedom of spirit and communion with God."[14]

In bringing our examination of early Methodist fasting to a close, it is helpful to summarize the key elements which made it significant. First and foremost, it was an act which glorified God by providing additional time for prayer. In the spiritual life, it was a tangible act which verified the truth of the priority of spirit over flesh. In this sense Wesley was not opposed to fasting standing as a protest to the self-indulgent practices of others in society, but never in a holier-than-thou attitude. Fasting stood for all to see as an act of reverence to God and proof that life could be lived temperately, keeping the material and spiritual dimensions in balance.

It may well be asked in our day if the same issues do not warrant the continued practice of fasting. We should look for any act of worship which leads to a greater glorification of God. In a society which often assigns value in terms of consumption, the example of self-denial is still noteworthy. Fasting is still a legitimate means of demonstrating the ultimacy of spiritual concerns. For the church, it could be now, as then, that God would bless corporate fasting with revival and renewal.

The Wesleyan tradition serves us well in restoring fasting to a place of significance in the spiritual life, all the while avoiding unnecessary and excessive practices. A mature spirituality will still do well to look for those occasions when we can lay aside attention to the body in order to give more attention to God.

Questions for Discussion

1. What new insights did you gain from this chapter? How do you plan to implement them in your ongoing spiritual formation?
2. Compare your own motives for fasting with those of Wesley in his purpose statement. What amendments need to be made? Why? What reasons have you heard others give for fasting which you feel need to be changed in light of this chapter?
3. What ideas do you have for restoring fasting to the whole church? Does corporate fasting have a place in the body of Christ today?

Chapter Six

Life Together

NO ONE CAN develop a mature spirituality alone. To be a Christian is to be called into community. It is to become a functioning part of the *body* of Christ. This fact has already been seen in the preceding chapters as each of the means of grace have had corporate expressions. But for Wesley, it was important to make the communal dimension of the spiritual life tangible for the early Methodists. He used the means of Christian conference to do it.

The term is not a familiar one today, but Wesley used it to describe all the group experiences which were provided through the United Societies. Our nearest parallel today would be the various forms of small group ministry existing inside and outside the institutional church. Wesley was able to view this dimension as a means of grace because he saw the principle exemplified in Jesus' calling together of the disciples and the New Testament emphases on assembly, koinonia, etc.

Through the variety of group ministries offered in the United Societies, Wesley saw certain key elements mediated: nurture, study, encouragement, stewardship, witness, and service. All of these needed to be present in the life of any believer, and they were best mediated through the group experience. In this chapter we want to examine the

54

several expressions of Christian conference, using them as a basis for implementing this means in spiritual formation today.

The largest unit of fellowship was the society. In places like Bristol and London the membership ran into the hundreds. But in many places they numbered less than a hundred. Between 1739 and 1743 these societies operated more or less independently, though Wesley's personal supervision assured consistency in the various groups. By 1743 it was obvious that some system was needed to coordinate the activities of the societies. So Wesley drew up the document known as *The General Rules of the United Societies.*

Membership in the societies was open to any person who wanted to flee the wrath to come. The society met weekly with prayer, exhortation, and mutual care being the chief components of their common life. The ultimate goal was to help one another work out their own salvation.[1] But it is important to see that this was no ingrown spirituality, for running along with it was a commitment to stewardship and ministry, also clearly spelled out in the *General Rules.*[2]

Wesley's motives in establishing the society structure have been variously interpreted. The dominant one seems to have been the realization that immediate nurture is needed for those who have been won by preaching. Going further, Wesley also made it clear that preaching alone could not produce mature spirituality. In the first year of the United Societies (1743) he wrote, "I determine, by the grace of God, not to strike one stroke in any place where I cannot follow the blow."[3] Twenty years later he visited an area where society meetings were in decline and afterward wrote,

I was more convinced than ever, that the preaching like an apostle, without joining together those that are awakened, and training them up in the ways of God, is only begetting children for the murderer. How much preaching there has been for these twenty years all over Pembrokeshire! But no regular societies, no discipline, no order or connection; and the consequence is, that nine in ten of the once-awakened are now faster asleep than ever.[4]

Related to nurture was the motive of renewal. Wesley had been influenced at Oxford in the 1730s by a work first published in 1680, *The Country Parson's Advice to His Parishioners.* In it the author declared,

If the good men of the Church will unite together in the several parts of the kingdom, disposing themselves into friendly societies, and engaging each other . . . in all good Christian ways, it will be the most effectual means for restoring our decaying Christianity to its primitive life and vigor.[5]

By 1743, a number of these religious societies had been formed.[6] Wesley's use of this form of group experience shows a similarity of spirit with those before him for the renewal of the church.

God confirmed Wesley's choice of the society structure as the basis for the early Methodist movement. By 1768, Methodism had 40 circuits and 27,341 members. Ten years later it had grown to 60 circuits and 40,089 members. Another decade later it had 99 circuits and 66,375 members. By 1798, Methodism had 149 circuits with 101,712 members.[7]

Wesley would be among the first to admit that the effectiveness of the United Societies lay in more than just the weekly mass meetings of the society. He knew by precept and example that spiritual formation requires small, more intimate fellowship than that. So the second level of group life was expressed in the class meetings.

Actually, the class-meeting concept developed more slowly. From 1739 to 1742, the emerging Methodist movement expressed itself primarily through the society and the band (to be discussed next in the order). In 1742, Wesley saw the need for an intermediate structure. This was necessary to provide for the continuation of personal nurture as the societies increased in size. This was especially important for those seekers in the society who were ineligible for membership in the bands. It was also necessary to provide geographical accessibility to the fellowship. By 1746, this dimension of group life had become an established part of the Methodist system.[8]

The class meeting comes as close to paralleling the contemporary small-group movement as any feature of Christian conference. Each group numbered approximately a dozen, who met in a home. Leaders were generally laymen, but laywomen are also known to have been in charge of groups. The class leaders were actually sub-pastors in the Methodist system, and some of the more prominent leaders itinerated over the area, making contact with all the classes.

In the beginning of the class-meeting movement the meetings tended to be more formal in nature, with the leader standing before the group asking questions about the spiritual condition of each member. However, the style became more relaxed and a family atmosphere prevailed. Leslie Church describes a typical meeting in these words:

> Problems were submitted and often solved, spir-
> itual experiences were shared, and the members

rejoiced in the conscious assurance of the presence of God. The meetings began and ended with a hymn and prayer, and there was simplicity and intimacy about the act of worship which any formalities would have destroyed.[9]

Besides fellowship, the class meeting also provided the basis for early Methodist stewardship and mission. "A penny a week and a shilling a quarter" became the rule.[10] Across the United Societies, this added up to a considerable sum, and the monies were primarily used to aid the poor and also to support traveling Methodist preachers.[11] It is also likely that this missional dimension helped keep the classes from becoming ingrown, spiritual admiration societies. Their ongoing life was an expression of Jesus' words, "to whom much is given, much is required."

The element of discipline is another noteworthy feature of the class meetings. Each member was given a class ticket which bore the person's name, the date, and the signature of Wesley or one of his preachers. The ticket was good for a quarter, and unfaithful members did not get their tickets renewed for the next quarter. Beyond the tickets, Wesley exercised further discipline through his periodic visits. At these he examined, regulated, and even purged the classes.[12]

By today's standards these practices seem harsh, but it would be a mistake to read any unloving or legalistic spirit into Wesley's practices. He was loved by his people too much for that, and they seem largely to have understood what he was doing. He was convinced that there could be no spiritual maturity without discipline. And besides, the classes were *voluntary* associations. No one was made to attend. Wesley expected members to obey the rules, not because they were forced to, but because they had chosen to. This explains why Wesley could purge the classes as necessary. He threw no one out. Members put themselves out by failing to observe the standards they had previously accepted. And we should always remember that readmittance was possible for anyone willing to reassume the rules of the group.

The result of all this was that the class meeting became the heart of the Methodist movement. During the eighteenth and nineteenth centuries it was the chief means of fellowship in British Methodism.[13] And interestingly, the classes seem to also have been the place where the greater number of conversions occurred.[14]

Although the long-term structure for Methodism was found in the society and class meetings, it is important to mention the bands. Wesley borrowed the idea for them from the Moravians, although they can be traced to a time even earlier than that.[15] Wesley utilized the band structure in the first societies, but by the time of his death in 1792, many bands no longer functioned and the class meeting came to dominate.

Attention must be given to the bands because of the underlying principle which gave rise to them. This was that spiritual maturity is fostered as persons of the same sex meet in very small, confidential meetings. So bands were organized for men and others for women. The average size was between five and eight, with none apparently larger than ten.

Rules for the bands were drawn up by Wesley in 1738, five years before the *General Rules of the United Societies* were developed. An examination of these rules indicates that the purpose of the weekly band meeting was for testimony and mutual examination. After a prayer and hymn, one person began the process of speaking the state of his or her soul. Then the rest, in order, likewise spoke concerning their state. Particular attention was given to overcoming personal faults and achieving a sense of forgiveness and peace with God.[16] It was a support group in the best sense of the word. Personal vulnerability was called for in specific ways. But the risk brought about a wave of mutual encouragement, counsel, and prayer.

Because of the intensive nature of the band experience, this was the only level of Methodist group life where members had to be professing Christians. Psychologically and theologically this is not hard to understand. Wesley knew that intimate, even risky sharing can only be done when one has settled the fundamental issue of being accepted by God. For one just outside the camp, or even marginally related to the movement, the experience could have been too threatening. Furthermore, the band meeting was also voluntary, and statistics indicate that only about twenty percent of Methodists took advantage of this form of spiritual formation.[17]

The societies, classes, and bands formed the major expressions of Methodist group life and served as a major means of grace in cultivating spiritual maturity. But they did not exhaust the system. Select societies (sometimes called select bands) existed for those who seemed to be making special progress in inward and outward holiness. Penitent groups also existed for those who had backslidden but were now ready to renew their commitment. And even beyond these regular meetings, the love feasts, watch nights, and covenant services provided less frequent opportunities for community life and growth.

Before drawing to a close, we should remember that everything which has been described is *in addition to* the regular services of the church. Early Methodism was, throughout Wesley's lifetime, a renewal movement within the Church of England. To be sure, many Anglican leaders did not support the Methodists. And the issue of Wesley's own relation to the established church is a complex issue beyond our ability to deal with it here. But the point must be made that early Methodism was not a substitute church for malcontents. More precisely, it was a church within the church offering levels of spirituality which were not being duplicated in the larger denomination. And besides involvement in the Methodist movement, Wesley fully expected his followers to be faithful members of their parish churches.

In our day there is a need to recover the experience of Christian conference within the church. I agree with those who believe that Methodism lost its heart when these dimensions were abandoned. I further believe that we would see a resurgence of vitality if we could rediscover the dynamic of relational ministries. People are hungry now as then for opportunities to personalize their Christian experience.

This will not mean a return to eighteenth-century models so much as it will mean a recovery of the principles which gave rise to the specific expressions of Christian conference. Among them the principle of voluntary association must always be kept in mind. Because we are starting as a church, not a movement, we must respect the right of persons not to opt for these special opportunities for group interaction. The fact that Wesley did this with respect to the bands is an historical example of wisdom which we cannot ignore. Nevertheless, we may be confident that enough will be interested to have vital group ministries within our churches.

Related to this will be the principle of variety. Group size, constituency, and purpose can be different. We may even want to allow for seekers as Wesley did within the group structure. And even where there is a similarity of format (e.g., home sharing groups), we can still allow for variety in the meetings from place to place.

A third principle highlights a uniting of group dynamics to ministry concerns. As groups form within the church, they should be challenged to look outside themselves for service projects. This may mean local concerns as well as a world vision, but it is this element of groups in ministry that prevents elitism and an ingrown spirit.

Fourth, we need to recover the potential of lay ministry. In every congregation there are those mature and willing men and women who can establish vital group ministries within the congregation. But like Wesley, we must not abandon them to such ministries. Training and continued oversight of the leadership core is a pastoral responsibility and privilege. And in the end it will mean an extension of ministry (beyond the ordained clergy) even as it did for Wesley.

If we choose this kind of Body-life structure for the church, we must insist upon discipline. If the presupposition of contemporary group ministries is voluntarism, then those who desire such fellowship must also be willing to commit to those disciplines which will make for spiritual maturation. At the least it will mean an attention to the classic, time-tested disciplines of the church.[18] It can also mean the implementation of legitimate disciplines which each church might adopt. But however it takes shape, we must return again to the conviction that without discipline the church will never achieve the maturity and power it is intended by God to have.

Finally, we will structure contemporary group ministries against the backdrop of fidelity to the larger church. We can rejoice when our people find experiences outside the traditional institutional expressions of corporate worship, Sunday school, connectional ministries, etc. But we should refuse to allow members to *substitute* the small group for the larger Body of Christ. Rather, we must bring the vitality of the group into the mainstream of institutional life. In this way, the energy of the group can find larger expression in the church, and the larger church will be enriched and renewed by the spiritual life coming to it from the group. If we are truly Wesleyan, cooperation—*not* competition—will characterize the relationship between the church and the groups within it. And where this is understood and practiced, Christian conference may again be discovered as an indispensable means of grace.

Questions for Discussion

1. Which of Wesley's forms of Christian conference appeals to you the most? Why?
2. What forms of group life do you have in your church? Do you see any Wesleyan principles undergirding them? Do you feel there are places where there is a need for such principles?
3. If your church does not have a group ministry, discuss how you might begin one. Develop a strategy that you might share with your pastor or administrative body.

Chapter Seven

Into the World

AS IMPORTANT and essential as the instituted means of grace were to John Wesley and the early Methodists, we would not likely have had a worldwide movement born by the use of these means alone. True enough, it has been shown that each of the particular means of grace had a community expression. That is good. But it is not sufficient to account for the impact early Methodism had on English society. And even more so, it is not sufficient to be a spiritual force to be contended with far beyond the shores of England. Something else was needed for this to happen. And for Wesleyan spirituality, that something was a concern for the prudential means of grace.

This term may at first be as unfamiliar as the term *instituted means of grace* was a few chapters earlier. Basically, Wesley meant that God had given additional means of grace to the church through which it fulfills the social and relational dimensions of the gospel. *Prudent* Christians would give attention to them as well as to the instituted means. Wesley wrote,

> It is generally supposed, that the means of grace, and the ordinances of God, are equivalent terms. We commonly mean by that expression, those

that are usually termed, works of piety; viz., hearing and reading the scripture, receiving the Lord's Supper, public and private prayer, and fasting. And it is certain that these are the ordinary channels which convey the grace of God to the souls of men. But are they the only means of grace? Are there no other means than these, whereby God is pleased, frequently, yea, ordinarily, to convey his grace to them that either love or fear him? Surely there are works of mercy, as well as works of piety, which are real means of grace.[1]

It is this linking of piety and mercy which gave Wesleyan spirituality its life and its ministry. It saved the United Societies from becoming ingrown and self-sufficient. Wesley made the world his parish and wanted his followers to do the same. Consequently, Wesley's interpreters nearly two hundred years later have seen his social ethic as an extension of his individual ethic.[2] Or to put it another way, here we see the Wesleyan synthesis—his ability to take two ideas which seem like opposites on the surface, and put them together to form a stronger unity than existed when they were kept separate.

This is exactly what happened in early Methodist spirituality. Their wedding of piety and mercy forged a more effective instrument in God's hand than they could ever have been if they had opted for one form of spirituality to the exclusion of the other. The same thing is true for our time. Holiness of heart *and* life remain the twin peaks of vital spirituality. So it is important for us to recognize the prudential means of grace.

Wesley sets them forth under three basic principles: doing no harm, doing good, and attending upon all the ordinances of God.[3] But he was wise enough to know that general principles alone are not usually sufficient to define or motivate ethics. So Wesley went farther in the *General Rules* and made lists of examples under each category. Some of the items in his lists are culturally and historically conditioned as we would expect. If he were making a similar list today, he would no doubt change it.

But to dismiss the basic principles because the lists seem outdated is to miss Wesley's point entirely. What he was trying to show was that social holiness (such as corporate ethics and acts of mercy) must be and can be expressed in specific ways. For our purposes this means that true spirituality is never *made spiritual*. Rather it is expressed through concrete acts of daily living.

Interestingly, the social dimension of spirituality can be expressed negatively as well as positively. It includes what we do *not* do, as well as what we do. "Doing no harm" brought the element of avoidance into the Christian's frame of reference. Our problem today is that this too easily seems like legalism. To read Wesley this way, however, is again to miss the point. Wesley's prohibitions were not binders so much as they were boundaries. He knew that antinomianism[4] resulted in spiritual inertia and moral chaos. He saw the use of law as necessary to guide the believer in the way of righteousness.[5]

The decades of the sixties and seventies have dealt a hard blow on this dimension of social and spiritual life. The relativity of morals and the stress on individual rights and privileges have seriously undercut our belief in universal standards of conduct. Our Wesleyan heritage, however, reminds us that such standards do exist. A vital spirituality will ask, "What do I need to be avoiding in my walk toward maturity in Christ?" Such a question will not arise out of any dualism,[6] nor will it be asked in order to limit our life. Rather, it will be asked as a means for *finding life*.

The social dimension comes in precisely at the point

that Wesley knew there was really no such thing as individual actions. Everything we say and do bears directly or indirectly upon another. The personal choice to avoid some things in life prevents others from becoming needlessly hurt and negatively influenced. The result is a positive effect upon society and a general uplifting of the quality of life.

The real thrust of Wesley's social spirituality, however, is its positive expression: "Doing good." Here too Wesley made a list of specific expressions, but he did so under three subcategories. First, he expected the Methodists to do good to the bodies of others. Here is the area which includes food, clothing, shelter, visiting the sick and prisoners. It is at this point that Wesley's affinity with the social relief ministries of our day can be seen.

Second, Wesley wanted them to do good to the souls of others. Under this category we can trace the Wesleyan motivation for evangelism and discipleship. Present also is the exhortation to sound teaching, in order to refute erroneous doctrines. For the purposes of this book it is important to trace this direct link between social spirituality and the concerns for redemption and nurture among those with whom we relate. Any spirituality which ignores the eternal destiny of others is foreign to the Wesleyan spirit. Furthermore, any spirituality which does not seek to reform erroneous theology is likewise foreign to the Wesleyan spirit. Here is another example of Wesley's synthesis of knowledge and vital piety.

Third, Wesley wanted this positive ethic to be shown "especially to them that are of the household of faith, or groaning so to be."[7] On the surface this might appear to be a bias toward preferential treatment, but Wesley's thrust is different. In a general society which Wesley would have certainly characterized as secular, it was his conviction that Christians should stick together. In other words, if social spirituality calls us to avoid evil and do good to *all* people, how much more we should be careful to apply this spirit to fellow Christians. Wesley put it this way: "The world will love its own, and them only."[8] Christians must show particular care for each other.

The third basic principle of Wesley's social spirituality was attendance upon all the ordinances of God. It is interesting that Wesley includes this list which is for the most part a repetition of the instituted means of grace. It seems that Wesley is doing two things at this point. First, he is grounding his social ethic in those elements which are not subject to cultural and historical adjustment. Specific examples of avoiding evil and doing good might change from generation to generation, but the instituted means are transcultural and transhistorical. It is these which give the social dimension of the gospel its roots.

Second, Wesley is effectively removing the ability to put things into neat, disconnected categories. By including a repeat of the instituted means within the discussion of the prudential means, he is showing how personal, corporate, and social spirituality overlap and interact. The result is a conjoining of factors which results in a much stronger whole than any single element could be on its own. And by doing so, Wesley will not allow us to rest until all these aspects are reflected in our spiritual formation.

This book began with a direct quotation from Wesley. It seems fitting to end it with one. As we think about a comprehensive view of spiritual life which Wesley had, and particularly (in this chapter) on its expression, these words seem particularly appropriate,

It is impossible for any that have it, to conceal
the religion of Jesus Christ. This our Lord makes

plain beyond all contradiction, by a two-fold comparison: "Ye are the light of the world: A city set upon a hill cannot be hid." Ye Christians are "the light of the world," with regard both to your tempers and actions. Your holiness makes you as conspicuous as the sun in the midst of heaven. As ye cannot go out of the world, so neither can ye stay in it without appearing to all mankind. . . . So impossible it is, to keep our religion from being seen, unless we cast it away. . . . Sure it is, that a secret, unobserved religion, cannot be the religion of Jesus Christ. Whatever religion can be concealed, is not Christianity.[9]

Questions for Discussion

1. Taking the two principles of "doing no harm" and "doing good," construct short, descriptive lists of what these principles might look like when expressed in our day.
2. If there are disagreements as to what should and should not be on the lists, what is the recourse for the Body? What light does this shed on Wesley's use of the instituted means of grace as a "rootage" for social spirituality?
3. Beginning with your household of faith, discuss ways you can express holiness of life (social spirituality, acts of mercy, etc.) toward others.
4. Reflect further upon Wesley's use of the instituted means of grace as the foundation for "doing no harm" and "doing good." What does this imply about social concerns today?

Postscript

The preceding chapters have largely been a presentation of Wesley's principles and practices in the spiritual life. I have intentionally avoided giving too much personal interpretation, choosing rather to illustrate the main ideas with material from Wesley himself and the early Methodists who followed him. I have adopted this method because I believe the knowledge of a tradition must precede the interpretation of it.

Unfortunately, this approach has not always been taken in Wesley Studies, and the result is that sometimes what goes under the name *Methodist* bears little resemblance to the tradition. Surely we owe it to ourselves to know what Wesley said and did in his time before we begin to project what he would say and do if he were alive today.

In this respect, I trust you as reader to make connections between Wesley and your own life. To try to make too many of those connections for you would rob you of the joy of discovering them for yourself. I believe that reflection upon the early expressions of our tradition can lead us to form contemporary expressions for our lives and the larger life of the church.

But having said that, I want to make it clear that a recovery of devotional life in the Wesleyan tradition will not and cannot mean a return to or simple repetition of the eighteenth century. There are some places where a recovery of specific practices is possible, even desirable. But there are other places where a recovery of the Wesleyan spirit (as Albert Outler calls it) will be the preferable route. But again, such a recovery (in practice or spirit) cannot be made apart from knowledge of the original.

I would encourage you to use this exposure to the Wesleyan tradition as motivation to dig deeper in your knowledge of Wesley's own words and actions. Unfortunately, the Jackson Edition of Wesley's works is not in print at the time of this writing (January 1983), but excerpts from Wesley's works are.[1] It will be this kind of reading which will enable you to think for yourself and draw your own conclusions about the desired shape of Wesleyanism in the future. I can also tell you that such a reading will be a richly rewarding experience and will certainly be an expression of your commitment to spiritual formation in the Wesleyan spirit.

When you have completed this examination, move into reputable secondary works.[2] These will help you flesh out your exposure to Wesley by providing helpful interpretation and by building insightful connections between facets of his life and thought. A final stage in this process can occur when you then begin to read the works which Wesley himself read.[3] This will help place Wesley (and you) in the larger stream of Christian thought.

An examination of Wesleyan spirituality is rewarding and possible for us today for the same reason it was for Wesley himself. We are on a common pilgrimage to renew scriptural Christianity. Allowing Wesley to speak one more time, we get a glimpse of what this means for spirituality:

> It is most true, that the root of religion lies in
> the heart, in the inmost soul; that this is the union

of the soul with God, the life of God in the soul of man. But if this root be really in the heart, it cannot but put forth branches [through] instances of outward obedience.[4]

We may be sure that as these features characterize our spiritual formation, we are practicing devotional life in the Wesleyan tradition.

Notes

Chapter One

1. John Telford, ed., *The Letters of the Rev. John Wesley* (1931; reprint, London: Epworth, 1960), 4:103.

2. All scripture references, unless otherwise noted, are from Wesley's *Explanatory Notes Upon the New Testament* (1954; reprint, Naperville, Ill.: Allenson, 1966).

3. Wesley's personal diary should not be confused with his published journal. The journal appears in his standard works. The diary is yet to appear in its complete text. Richard Heitzenrater is currently transcribing Wesley's diaries for publication in the new edition of Wesley's works (*The Works of John Wesley*, New York: Oxford, 1975-) currently going forward under the editorship of Dr. Frank Baker.

4. Theodore W. Jennings, *Life as Worship: Prayer and Praise in Jesus' Name* (Grand Rapids: Eerdmans, 1982), pp. 25-30.

5. A helpful booklet dealing with the problem of spiritual dryness is Walter Trobisch's *Spiritual Dryness* (Downers Grove, Ill.: Inter-Varsity, 1970).

6. Nehemiah Curnock, ed., *The Journal of the Rev. John Wesley* (1909; reprint, London: Epworth, 1938), 5:169.

7. Perhaps the best-known favorites of Wesley were Thomas à Kempis's *The Imitation of Christ*, William Law's *A Serious Call to a Devout and Holy Life*, and Jeremy Taylor's *Holy Living* and *Holy Dying*. For an extensive list of Wesley's devotional reading consult my Ph.D. dissertation, "The Devotional Life of John Wesley: 1703-38" (Durham, N.C.: Duke University, 1981).

8. Several works are helpful in coming to know the classics of devotion. Doubleday has published three volumes entitled, *The Doubleday Devotional Classics* (E. Glenn Hinson, ed., 1978). Baker Book House has reprinted Thomas Kepler's *Anthology of Devotional Literature* (1977). The Upper Room has published a series of booklets entitled *Living Selections from the Great Devotional Classics.*

9. One of the finest examples of Wesley's use of letters to guide another's spiritual growth is the thirty-seven-letter set of correspondence between himself and "Miss March." (Telford, *Letters* 4:100, 109, 157, 180, & 310; and 5:82, 192, & 261-65 are some of the major letters.) In one of the letters (5:193) Wesley declares that he wants only to "say just what I hope may direct your goings in the way and prevent your being weary or faint in your mind."

10. This theme is developed further in chapter 6.

11. Francis Gerald Ensley, *John Wesley, Evangelist* (Nashville: Methodist Evangelistic Materials, 1958), p. 47.

12. Colin W. Williams, *John Wesley's Theology Today* (Nashville: Abingdon, 1960), p. 158.

13. Frank Baker's *John Wesley and the Church of England* (Nashville: Abingdon, 1970) is one of the best treatments of Wesley's relationship to the Anglican Church.

Chapter Two

1. Henri J. M. Nouwen, *Creative Ministry* (Garden City, N.Y.: Doubleday, 1971), xviii.

2. Thomas Jackson, ed., *The Works of John Wesley* (Grand Rapids: Baker Book House, 1979), 8:322-24. At the present time this edition is considered the standard edition in Wesley Studies. Hereafter it will simply be referred to as *Works.*

3. Telford, *Letters* 4:90.

4. Jackson, *Works* 6:81. Sermon, "The Wilderness State."

5. Jackson, *Works* 5:192.

6. These themes are illustrated in Wesley's first publication, *A Collection of Forms of Prayer for Every Day in the Week* (1733). Sunday—Love of God; Monday—Love of Neighbor; Tuesday—Humility;

Wednesday—Mortification; Thursday—Resignation and Meekness; Friday—Mortification; and Saturday—Thankfulness. The text for these prayers is found in *Works* 11:203-37.

7. Wesley indicated places for extemporaneous praying by the use of parentheses within written prayers.

8. Anthony Bloom, *Beginning to Pray* (New York: Paulist, 1970).

9. Norman Vincent Peale, *How to Have a Good Day Every Day* (Pawling, N.Y.: Foundation for Christian Living, 1980), p. 5.

10. Wesley, *Notes Upon the New Testament*, p. 762. 1 Thessalonians 5:16-17.

11. Before Wesley published *A Collection of Forms of Prayer for Every Day in the Week* in 1733, he used a handwritten notebook to collect the prayers of others and use them as aids to his own praying. I have transcribed this prayer manual from Wesley's abbreviated shorthand and included it in my Ph.D. dissertation, "The Devotional Life of John Wesley: 1703-38."

Chapter Three

1. John Wesley, *Standard Sermons, Consisting of Forty-Four Discourses published in four volumes . . .* (London: Epworth, 1967), vi.

2. Wesley, *Standard Sermons*, vi.

3. For further reading about the place and significance of the Bible in the Wesleyan tradition, see Mack B. Stokes's *The Bible in the Wesleyan Heritage* (Nashville: Abingdon, 1979).

4. Wesley, *Standard Sermons*, vi.

5. *Explanatory Notes Upon the New Testament* was first published in 1755. *Explanatory Notes Upon the Old Testament* appeared in 1765. The New Testament notes came to stand, along with *Standard Sermons* and *Articles of Religion*, as the doctrinal standards of British and American Methodism.

6. Wesley, *Notes Upon the New Testament*, p. 6.

7. John Wesley, *Explanatory Notes Upon the Old Testament* (Bristol: William Pine, 1765; Salem, Ohio: Schmul, 1975), 1:viii.

8. Wesley, *Notes Upon the Old Testament*, viii.

9. Wesley, *Notes Upon the Old Testament*, viii.

10. Paul Little, *How to Give Away Your Faith* (Chicago: Inter-Varsity, 1966), pp. 126-27.

11. Wesley, *Standard Sermons*, vi.

12. Wesley, *Notes Upon the New Testament*, p. 794.

13. Jackson, *Works* 8:269-71.

14. Jackson, *Works* 8:275-338. See also an article by George Turner, "John Wesley as an Interpreter of Scripture" in *Inspiration and Interpretation*, edited by John F. Walvoord (Grand Rapids: Eerdmans, 1957), p. 174.

15. The new edition of Wesley's works edited by Frank Baker will contain a volume of representative Wesleyan hymnody. Numerous references to scripture are supplied to help the reader see the Wesleys' indebtedness to the Bible in their hymns.

16. William Vermillion, "The Devotional Use of Scripture in the Wesleyan Movement," *Wesleyan Theological Journal*, 16, no. 1 (1981):59.

Chapter Four

1. Albert C. Outler, ed., *John Wesley* (New York: Oxford University Press, 1964), p. 333.

2. George Osborn, comp., *The Poetical Works of John and Charles Wesley* (London: Wesleyan-Methodist conference office, 1869), 3:186.

3. Jackson, *Works* 1:280.

4. Jackson, *Works* 1:279.

5. *The Methodist Hymnal*, (Nashville: Methodist Publishing House, 1964), #830.

6. Outler, *John Wesley*, p. 33.

7. Jackson, *Works* 7:148.

8. Jackson, *Works* 7:152.

9. Jackson, *Works* 7:154.

10. Jackson, *Works* 7:150.

11. Jackson, *Works* 7:149.

12. Jackson, *Works* 1:280.

13. Quoted in Outler's *John Wesley,* p. 415.

14. Jackson, *Works* 7:156.

15. Jackson, *Works* 7:209.

16. Telford, *Letters* 7:239.

17. Frank Baker, *John Wesley and the Church of England* (Nashville: Abingdon, 1970), p. 157. The issue of whom to allow at the Lord's Supper is complicated by Wesley's views regarding the doubtful value of confirmation. Further insight into this particular issue is possible by reading in Baker's work, pp. 236, 244, and 331.

Chapter Five

1. Wesley, *Notes Upon the New Testament,* p. 39.

2. Jackson, *Works* 5:345.

3. Jackson, *Works* 5:346.

4. Jackson, *Works* 5:346-47.

5. Jackson, *Works* 5:346.

6. Jackson, *Works* 5:359.

7. Jackson, *Works* 5:348-51.

8. Frank Baker, ed., *The Works of John Wesley* (New York: Oxford University Press, 1975), 11:79. Unit editor for volume 11 was Gerald R. Cragg.

9. Jackson, *Works* 5:357-58.

10. John Wesley, *The Nature, Design, and General Rules of the United Societies in London, Bristol, Kingswood and Newcastle upon Tyne, & c.* (Newcastle-Upon-Tyne: Printed by John Gooding, on the Side, 1743), p. 8. Cf. Jackson, *Works* 8:271.

11. "Conference Minutes of 1744," *Publications of the Wesley Historical Society,* No. 1 (London: C. H. Kelly, 1896), p. 17.

12. Leslie Frederic Church, *More About the Early Methodist People* (London: Epworth, 1949), p. 278.

13. Telford, *Letters* 5:112.

14. John Parker, ed., *Memoirs of Miss Hannah Ball of High Wycombe* (London: Mason, 1839), pp. 39-40.

Chapter Six

1. Wesley, *General Rules*, p. 1. Cf. Jackson, *Works* 8:267.

2. Wesley, *General Rules*, pp. 5-8, and Jackson, *Works* 8: 270-71. These elements of mission and ministry will be discussed in the next chapter.

3. Jackson, *Works* 1:416.

4. Jackson, *Works* 3:144.

5. Samuel Emerick, ed., *Spiritual Renewal for Methodism* (Nashville: Methodist Evangelistic Materials, 1958), p. 12.

6. One of the best sources for studying this development is John S. Simon's *John Wesley and the Religious Societies* (London: Epworth, 1921).

7. Howard Snyder, *The Radical Wesley* (Downers Grove, Ill.: Inter-Varsity, 1980), p. 54.

8. Emerick, *Spiritual Renewal*, pp. 17-18.

9. Church, *Early Methodist People*, p. 236.

10. Snyder, *Radical Wesley*, p. 55.

11. Abel Stevens, *The History of the Religious Movement of the Eighteenth Century, Called Methodism, Considered in its Different Denominational Forms, and its Relations to British and American Protestantism* (New York: Carlton and Porter, 1858-1861), 2:454.

12. Snyder, *Radical Wesley*, p. 57.

13. Emerick, *Spiritual Renewal*, p. 18.

14. Emerick, *Spiritual Renewal*, p. 25.

15. Martin Schmidt, *John Wesley: A Theological Biography* vols. (Nashville: Abingdon, 1963), 1:267.

16. Jackson, *Works* 8:272-73.

17. "Note by Mr. George Stampe," *Proceedings of the Wesley Historical Society*, V, No. 2 (1905), pp. 33-44.

18. Richard J. Foster, *Celebration of Discipline* (New York: Harper and Row, 1978), contains one of the best and most widely read discussions of the spiritual disciplines of any contemporary work.

Chapter Seven

1. Jackson, *Works* 7:117.
2. Robert W. Burtner & Robert E. Chiles, *John Wesley's Theology: A Collection from his Works* (Nashville: Abingdon, 1982), p. 223.
3. Wesley, *General Rules*, pp. 5-9.
4. Antinomianism is the belief that a person or group is not obligated to keep the law. In Wesley's day it pertained to certain groups who believed that, because they were under grace, they were freed from works of the law. Wesley saw this belief as dangerous, creating at best an amorality, but more often actual immorality.
5. Jackson, *Works* 5:433-46.
6. Dualism as used here refers to a belief which sees the material dimension of life as evil and the spiritual dimension as good. Wesley knew that this approach to spirituality too often results in unnatural asceticism. Therefore, he put the negative ethic of doing no harm on another basis.
7. Wesley, *General Rules*, p. 7.
8. Wesley, *General Rules*, p. 7.
9. Jackson, *Works* 5:301-2.

Postscript

1. Among the best and most accessible sources are the work by Burtner and Chiles (previously cited), the study by Albert Outler called *John Wesley* (previously cited), and *The Heart of Wesley's Journal* (Keats Publishing Co., 1979). *Wesley's Fifty-Two Standard Sermons* is available from Schmul Publishing Co. His *Explanatory Notes Upon the New Testament* have recently been reprinted by Baker Book House. Discipleship Resources has also published two sets of leaflets entitled *Saddlebags of Sermons and Other Works by John Wesley* which contain excerpts from some of the major sermons of Wesley.
2. Look back over the notes at the end of each chapter. You will find a number of good secondary materials. Added to this, you might want to have my book, *John Wesley's Message for Today*,

published by Zondervan. It will give you an introduction to Wesley's theology by examining his "order of salvation." Helpful bibliographies can be found in Outler's *John Wesley* and Williams's *John Wesley's Theology Today*.

3. At the present time, a good list of what Wesley read is found in the out-of-print work by V. H. H. Green, *The Young Mr. Wesley* (1961, published by various publishers). It documents his reading through 1734. Richard Heitzenrater's dissertation, "John Wesley and the Oxford Methodists" (Duke University, 1972) has a better and more accurate list which goes through 1735. My dissertation, "The Devotional Life of John Wesley" extends the list to 1738. From these lists you will be able to find literally hundreds of devotional works, many of which you can still find today. Also, refer to footnote #8 for chapter 1 for a list of several devotional classics. Finally, you will want to follow the series, *Classics of Western Spirituality* (Paulist Press). There is a good volume devoted to the spirituality of John and Charles Wesley, as well as a number of others which Wesley read.

4. Jackson, *Works* 5:303-4.